THE LITTLE BOOK OF
LOVE

Published by OH!
20 Mortimer Street
London W1T 3JW

Text © 2020 OH!
Design © 2020 OH!

Disclaimer:
All trademarks, quotations, company names, registered names,
products, characters, logos and catchphrases used or cited in this
book are the property of their respective owners. This book is a
publication of OH! An imprint of Welbeck Publishing Group
Limited and has not been licensed, approved, sponsored, or
endorsed by any person or entity. All rights reserved. No part of
this publication may be reproduced, stored in a retrieval system,
or transmitted in any form or by any means (including electronic,
mechanical, photocopying, recording, or otherwise) without prior
written permission from the publisher.

ISBN 978-1-91161-099-1

Compiled by: Victoria Godden
Project manager: Russell Porter
Design: James Pople
Production: Rachel Burgess

A CIP catalogue for this book is available from the Library of Congress

Printed in Dubai

10 9 8 7 6 5 4 3 2

Illustrations: freepik.com

THE LITTLE BOOK OF
LOVE

WORDS FROM THE HEART

CONTENTS

INTRODUCTION

Romantic, familial, platonic or epic – love connects all who have felt its warm embrace.

It was Plato who said that "At the touch of love, everyone becomes a poet", and this would certainly explain the breadth and depth of thought and consideration given to the subject over the centuries. Indeed, one could say that no other topic has inspired such beauty – in art, literature, poetry or music.

From Shakespeare's sonnets to the rom-coms of modern-day cinema, Enlightenment philosophy to the latest Nicholas Sparks novel, we can't help but continue to look for new ways to express the inexpressible when it comes to love, and this little book is testament to that, containing a relatively tiny selection of what must amount to millions of words devoted to the subject.

In these pages you will find the words of civil rights activists alongside those of movie stars, world leaders and the philosophers of Ancient Greece. As well as some of the most poignant reflections on the power of love, the experience of being head over heels in love, and some hard-won lovers' wisdom, there is also a plethora of interesting facts and stats about the big L. In addition, a whole chapter is dedicated to the most famous, endearing and enduring declarations of love ever spoken or committed to the page.

This is a book for the lovesick and the heartbroken, those lucky enough to have found love and those who have not given up hope of finding it.

CHAPTER
ONE

The Power of Love

Love can make us feel invincible, untouchable, on top of the world. But it can just as easily make us sick with heartache.

Love has the power to bring people together, to brighten our day and give meaning to our life.

Indeed, after reading the following pages, one might ask whether there is anything that love *can't* do...

66

Love recognizes no
barriers. It jumps hurdles,
leaps fences, penetrates
walls to arrive at its
destination full of hope.

99

Maya Angelou

66

Darkness cannot
drive out darkness, only
light can do that. Hate
cannot drive out hate, only
love can do that.

99

Martin Luther King Jr.

"

Death cannot stop
true love.
All it can do is delay it
for a while.

"

Westley,
The Princess Bride **(1987)**

love (n.)

from the Old English *lufu*, of Germanic origin; from an Indo-European root shared by Sanskrit *lubhyati* "desires", Latin *libet* "it is pleasing", libido "desire", also by the noun *leave* and *lief*.

Source: **Oxford Learner's Dictionary**

66

Where there is love
there is life.

99

**Mahatma
Gandhi**

66

Love is the only
sane and satisfactory
answer to the problem of
human existence.

99

Erich Fromm

66

Who, being loved, is poor?

99

Hester, Oscar Wilde's
A Woman of No Importance (1893)

"

Whoso loves
believes the impossible.

"

Elizabeth Barrett Browning

In the original French version of the fortune-telling game "He Loves Me... He Loves Me Not", typically played with daisies, each petal represented not just whether the player was loved by their amour, but how much: un peu *("a little")*, beaucoup *("a lot")*, passionnément *("passionately")*, à la folie *("to madness"), or* pas du tout *("not at all").*

66

Being deeply loved by someone gives you strength, while loving someone deeply gives you courage.

99

Lao-Tzu

66

One word frees us
of all the weight and pain
of life:
That word is love.

99

Sophocles

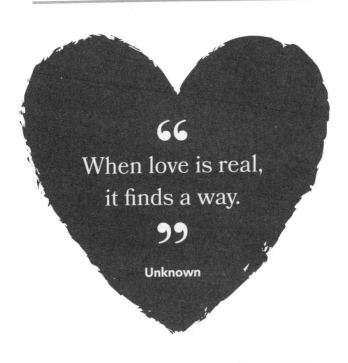

66
When love is real,
it finds a way.

99

Unknown

66

What greater thing is there for two
human souls, than to feel
that they are joined for life –
to strengthen each other in all labor,
to rest on each other in all sorrow,
to minister to each other in all
pain, to be one with each other in
silent unspeakable memories at the
moment of the last parting?

99

George Eliot, *Adam Bede*, (1859)

"

Age does not protect you
from love but love,
to some extent, love protects
you from age.

"

Jeanne Moreau

66

Love is not love
Which alters when it
alteration finds,

Or bends with the remover
to remove:

O no! it is an ever-fixed mark

That looks on tempests and
is never shaken ...

99

**William Shakespeare,
"Sonnet 116", (1609)**

In 2012, a man named Alexey Bykov faked his own death, right in front of his girlfriend, as part of an elaborate marriage proposal.

She said yes.

"

Love and compassion
are necessities, not
luxuries.
Without them humanity
cannot survive.

"

Dalai Lama

True love
**cannot be found
where it truly does not exist,
nor can it be**
hidden
where it
truly does.

Top 5 Bestselling
Love Songs
of All Time

1. **"Love is All Around"**
   Wet Wet Wet (1994)

2. **"Unchained Melody"**
   Robson and Jerome (1995)

3. **"(Everything I Do) I Do It For You"**
   Bryan Adams (1991)

4. **"Anything Is Possible/Evergreen"**
   Will Young (2001)

5. **"I Will Always Love You"**
   Whitney Houston (2002)

Source: **officialcharts.com**

66

We are most alive
when we're in love.

99

John Updike

Soul meets soul on
lovers' lips.

Percy Bysshe Shelley,
Prometheus Unbound **(1820)**

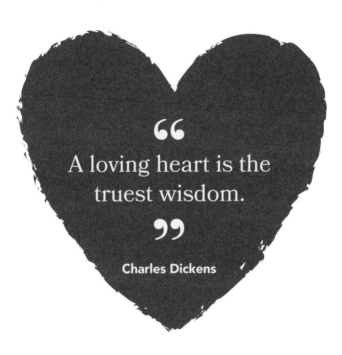

A loving heart is the truest wisdom.

Charles Dickens

66

Love casts out fear.

99

Louisa May Alcott,
Little Women **(1868)**

The world's oldest known love poem was thought to be written around 4,000 years ago. Etched on a clay tablet in southern Iraq, it was titled "Istanbul #2461" by the archaeologists who found it.

(See page 150 for the first verse)

CHAPTER
TWO

Lovers' Wisdom

Whether we like it or not, we
all need advice from time to time
when it comes to the ways and
wiles of love.

These words of wisdom,
hard-won or gained through a
lifetime of experience, will guide
you, inspire you and keep
the course of love running, if not
smooth, then at least a little
less bumpy...

66

Pleasure of love
lasts but a moment.
Pain of love
lasts a lifetime.

99

Bette Davis

"

Tis better to have loved
and lost, than never to have
loved at all.

"

**Alfred, Lord Tennyson,
"In Memoriam A.H.H." (1850)**

66

To love or have loved,
that is enough.
Ask nothing further.
There is no other pearl
to be found in the dark
folds of life.

99

Victor Hugo,
Les Miserables **(1862)**

Only in the
agony of parting
do we look
into the depths
of love.

Queen Victoria mourned Prince Albert's death for forty years, instead of the conventional two. She never remarried and continued to have a set of his clothes laid out every morning until her death in 1901.

Source: **HistoryExtra**

You may only be
one person
to the world, but you
may also be
the world
to one person.

"

Love
is an ideal thing,
marriage
a real thing.

"

Goethe

> **66**
>
> I have decided to
> stick to love;
> hate is too great a burden
> to bear.
>
> **99**

Martin Luther King Jr.

Why do we make
a division between straight
and gay?
Isn't love just love,
no matter what
gender?

"

When one is in love, one always begins by deceiving one's self, and one always ends by deceiving others. That is what the world calls a romance.

"

Oscar Wilde,
The Picture of Dorian Gray (1890)

66

The course of
true love never did run
smooth.

99

Shakespeare,
A Midsummer Night's
Dream, Act I, Scene 2

When a man wants to marry a woman in Fiji, the prospective groom must present the father of the intended bride with a sperm whale's tooth. Traditionally, he would have had to fight the world's largest mammal for it – so it was a good way to tell if he was serious or not!

"
You don't need
scores of suitors.
You need
only one, if he's the
right one.
"

Amy,
Little Women (1994)

66

A simple 'I love you' means
more than money.

99

Frank Sinatra

66

If I could but know
his heart,
everything would
become easy.

99

**Marianne Dashwood,
Jane Austen's *Sense and Sensibility* (1811)**

66

The greatest
thing you'll ever learn
is just to love,
and be
loved in return.

99

Tolouse, *Moulin Rouge* **(2001)**

10 Ways to Say
"I Love You"
Around the World

Te quiero

Ya lyublyu tebya

Je t'aime

Ich liebe dich

Ti amo

Ég elska þig

愛してる

我喜欢你

Σε αγαπώ

אנא בהוא אותר

66

A fool in love makes
no sense to me.
I only think you are a fool
if you do not love.

99

Unknown

66

It doesn't matter
if the guy is perfect or the
girl is perfect,
as long as they are perfect
for each other.

99

Sean, *Good Will Hunting* (1997)

"

In my opinion,
the best thing you can do
is find someone
who loves you for exactly
what you are.
Good mood, bad mood,
ugly, pretty, handsome,
what have you.

"

Mac MacGuff, *Juno* (2007)

The best thing to hold onto in life is each other.

Audrey Hepburn

66

When you love someone,
you love the person
as they are, and not as you'd
like them to be.

99

Leo Tolstoy

66

If you would be loved,
love and be lovable.

99

Benjamin Franklin,
Poor Richard's Almanac **(1755)**

*Pope Gelasius declared
14 February St Valentine's Day,
some believe because he wanted to
"Christianize" the pagan festival
Lupercalia, which was celebrated
on the 15th of the month.*

66

The greatest
happiness of life is the
conviction that we are loved;
loved for ourselves,
or rather, loved in spite of
ourselves.

99

Victor Hugo

66

The real lover
is the man who can thrill
you by kissing your
forehead or smiling into
your eyes or just
staring into space.

99

Marilyn Monroe

66

Never love anyone
who treats you like you're
ordinary.

99

Oscar Wilde

You don't
love a woman
because she's
beautiful;

she is
beautiful
because
you
love her.

The
8 Types of Love
(according
to the Ancient Greeks)

1. Eros (romantic, passionate love)

2. Philia (affectionate love)

3. Agape (selfless, universal love)

4. Storge (familiar love)

5. Mania (obsessive love)

6. Ludus (playful love)

7. Pragma (enduring love)

8. Philautia (self-love)

66

We learn
only from those
we love.

99

Johann Von Eckermann

66

Love yourself first and everything falls into line.

99

Lucille Ball

❝

The three hardest tasks
in the world are neither physical
feats nor intellectual
achievements, but moral acts:
1) To return love for hate;
2) To include the excluded; and
3) To say 'I was wrong.'

❞

Ernst Heinrich Haeckel

"

Some love stories
aren't epic novels.
Some are short stories.
But that doesn't make them
any less filled with love.

"

Carrie Bradshaw,
Sex and the City **(2008)**

"

If you find someone you
love in your life, then hang
on to that love.

"

Princess Diana

66

Your task is not to
seek for love, but merely to
seek and find
all the barriers within
yourself that you have
built against it.

99

Rumi

The
word
"love"
appears
310 times
in the
King James
Bible.

66

Above all,
love each other deeply,
because love
covers over a multitude
of sins.

99

**1 Peter 4:8,
New International Version**

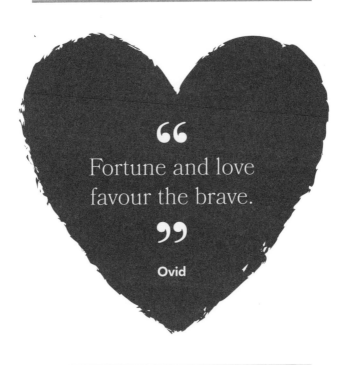

"
Fortune and love
favour the brave.
"

Ovid

"

There is no happiness like
that of being loved
by your fellow-creatures,
and feeling that your
presence is an addition
to their comfort.

"

Charlotte Brontë, *Jane Eyre* (1847)

66

It is not every man's fate
to marry the woman who
loves him best.

99

Jane Austen, *Emma* **(1815)**

CHAPTER
THREE

What Is Love?

Ah, the eternal question!

Can we ever pinpoint exactly what this thing we call "love" is? Can we describe its very essence, its very nature? Or are metaphors all we can hope for?

We may never truly understand it, but that hasn't stopped us trying over the centuries, as the following descriptions of love will attest...

66

Love is composed
of a single soul inhabiting
two bodies.

99

Aristotle

Love
knows no
gender.

"

Love is a possible
strength
in an actual weakness.

,,

Thomas Hardy,
Far from the Madding Crowd **(1874)**

"

Love is that condition
in the healing spirit
so profound that it allows
us to forgive.

"

Maya Angelou

Shakespeare's plays feature
the word "love" 1,640 times,
ten times more than "hate"
(163 times).

“

Love alters not with his brief hours
and weeks,

But bears it out even to the
edge of doom.

If this be error and upon
me prov'd,

I never writ, nor no man
ever lov'd.

”

**William Shakespeare,
"Sonnet 116" (1609)**

Love is like
quicksilver in the hand.
Leave the fingers
open and it stays. Clutch it,
and it darts away.

"

There is always some madness in love. But there is also always some reason in madness.

"

Nietzsche,
Thus Spake Zarathustra **(1883–1885)**

66

Love is a great
beautifier.

99

Louisa May Alcott,
Little Women
(1868)

"

Love seeketh not itself to please,

Nor for itself hath any care;

But for another gives its ease,

And builds a Heaven in Hell's despair.

"

William Blake,
"The Clod and the Pebble" (1794)

"

Love is a spirit
all compact of fire.

"

**Shakespeare,
"Venus and Adonis" (1593)**

10 Iconic Loves
of Literature

Elizabeth and Mr Darcy – *Pride and Prejudice*

Romeo and Juliet – *Romeo and Juliet*

Paris and Helen – *The Iliad*

Cathy and Heathcliff *Wuthering Heights*

Mark Anthony and Cleopatra –
Antony and Cleopatra

Jane and Mr Rochester – *Jane Eyre*

Tristan and Isolde – *Tristan and Iseuld*

Lancelot and Guinevere – *Le Morte d'Arthur*

Scarlett and Rhett – *Gone With the Wind*

Jay and Daisy – *The Great Gatsby*

66

Love is patient, love is kind.
It does not envy, it does not boast, it is
not proud. It does not dishonor others,
it is not self-seeking, it is not easily
angered, it keeps no record of wrongs.
Love does not delight in evil but
rejoices with the truth.
It always protects, always trusts,
always hopes, always perseveres.
Love never fails.

99

1 Corinthians 13:4–8,
New International Version

"

Love is passion,
obsession,
someone you can't live
without.

"

William Parrish, *Meet Joe Black* (1998)

The Ancient Greeks thought that orchids
were powerful aphrodisiacs.
They would grind them up and add
them to wine, believing that the love
potion would inspire passionate love in
the one who drank from it.

"

...when Love speaks,
the voice of all the gods

Makes heaven drowsy with
the harmony.

"

Biron,
Shakespeare's *Love's Labour's*
***Lost*, Act IV, Scene 3**

66

Love is friendship that has caught fire.

99

Ann Landers

"

Lovers
don't finally meet
somewhere.
They're in each other
all along.

"

Rumi

66

Love is blind and lovers
cannot see...

99

**Jessica,
Shakespeare's *The Merchant of Venice*,
Act II, Scene 6**

10 Animals That
Mate For Life

Macaroni penguins   Shingleback skinks

Sandhill cranes   Bald eagles

Seahorses   Gibbons

Gray wolves   Swans

Barn owls   Beavers

CHAPTER
FOUR

Head Over Heels

We know it when we feel it – that totally over-the-top, so-in-love-it-hurts feeling of being completely and utterly *smitten*.

Being in love is a strange experience, and words sometimes have a hard time describing it.

Nevertheless, romance has a way of making wordsmiths of us all...

66

I fell in love
the way you fall asleep:
slowly, and then
all at once.

99

Hazel Grace Lancaster,
The Fault in Our Stars **(2014)**

> **"** The heart has its reasons of which reason knows nothing. **"**

Blaise Pascal

66

You can't blame gravity for falling in love.

99

Albert Einstein

66

Their eyes instantly met,
and the cheeks of both
were overspread with the
deepest blush.

99

Jane Austen, *Pride and Prejudice* (1813)

Falling in love
triggers the same sensation
of euphoria
experienced by people when
they take cocaine.

Source: **Medical News Today**

"

If music be the food of love,
play on;

Give me excess of it, that, surfeiting,

The appetite may sicken,
and so die.

"

**Duke Orsino,
Shakespeare's *Twelfth Night*,
Act I, Scene 1**

66

My love for Linton
is like the foliage in the woods:
time will change it, I'm well aware,
as winter changes the trees.
My love for Heathcliff resembles
the eternal rocks beneath:
a source of little visible delight,
but necessary.

99

Cathy,
Emily Brontë's *Wuthering Heights* (1847)

"

You know you're in love
when you can't fall asleep
because the reality
is finally better than
your dreams.

"

Dr Seuss

“

Let him kiss me with the
kisses of his mouth –

for your love is more
delightful than wine.

”

**Song of Songs 1:2,
New International Version**

66

I love her,
and that's the beginning
and end
of everything.

99

**F. Scott Fitzgerald
(about his wife, Zelda)**

66

He stepped down,
trying not to
look long at her, as if
she were the sun,
yet he saw her, like the sun,
even without looking.

99

Leo Tolstoy, *Anna Karenina* (1877)

The
word

"LOVE"

is mentioned
102 times
in the Beatles' hit
1967 song
"All You Need is Love".

66

It was many and many a year ago,

In a kingdom by the sea,

That a maiden there lived whom
you may know

By the name of Annabel Lee;

And this maiden she lived with
no other thought

Than to love and be loved
by me.

99

Edgar Allan Poe, *Annabel Lee* (1849)

66

They say when you
meet the love of your life,
time stops,
and that's true.

99

Edward Bloom, *Big Fish* (2003)

"

If I loved you less,
I might be able to talk
about it more.

"

**Knightley,
Jane Austen's *Emma* (1815)**

66

But soft, what light through yonder window breaks?

It is the east, and Juliet is the sun.

Arise, fair sun, and kill the envious moon,

Who is already sick and pale with grief

That thou, her maid, art far more fair than she.

99

Romeo, Shakespeare's
***Romeo and Juliet*, Act II, Scene 2**

10 Best
On-Screen Romances

Jerry Maguire and Dorothy Boyd (*Jerry Maguire*)

Rose Dewitt Bukater and Jack Dawson (*Titanic*)

Ilsa Lund and Rick Blaine (*Casablanca*)

Allie and Noah (*The Notebook*)

Ennis Del Mar and Jack Twist (*Brokeback Mountain*)

Buttercup and Westley (*The Princess Bride*)

Sandy and Danny (*Grease*)

Alabama Whitman and Clarence Worley (*True Romance*)

Anna Scott and William Thacker (*Notting Hill*)

Scarlett O'Hara and Rhett Butler (*Gone With the Wind*)

66

At his lips' touch
she blossomed like
a flower
and the incarnation
was complete.

99

Nick Carraway,
F. Scott Fitzgerald's *The Great Gatsby*
(1925)

"

I love how she
makes me feel like anything
is possible, or like life
is worth it.

"

Tom Hansen,
***500 Days of Summer* (2009)**

66

Whatever our souls are made of, his and mine are the same.

99

Cathy,
Emily Brontë's *Wuthering Heights* (1847)

66

She walks in beauty, like the night

Of cloudless climes and
starry skies;

And all that's best of dark
and bright

Meet in her aspect and
her eyes...

99

Lord Byron, "She Walks in Beauty" (1814)

66

I am in love – and, my God,
it is the greatest thing that can
happen to a man.
I tell you, find a woman
you can fall in love with. Do it.
Let yourself fall in love.
If you have not done so already,
you are wasting your life.

99

D. H. Lawrence

> 66
>
> I wonder, by my troth,
> what thou and I
> Did, till we loved?
>
> 99

John Donne, "The Good-Morrow" (1633)

The Greek God of Love
is Eros
(from which the word "erotic"
originates).

His Roman equivalent
is Cupid.

"

I've fallen in love.
I'm an ordinary woman.
I didn't think
such violent things
could happen to
ordinary people.

"

Laura Jesson,
Brief Encounter **(1945)**

66

The very instant that I saw you did

My heart fly to your service...

99

**Ferdinand,
Shakespeare's *The Tempest*,
Act III, Scene 1**

"

It's like in that moment
the whole universe existed
just to bring us together.

"

Jonathan Trager, *Serendipity* **(2001)**

My beloved is mine
and I am his.

**Song of Songs 2:16,
New International
Version**

Top 10
Depictions of Love in Art

"The Kiss", Klimt

"The Jewish Bride", Rembrandt

"The Kiss", Auguste Rodin

**"Lovers in the Snow under an Umbrella",
Suzuki Harunobu**

"Kiss by the Hôtel de Ville", Robert Doisneau

"Le Printemps (Springtime)", Pierre-Auguste Cot

"The Kiss", Francesco Hayez

"We Rose Up Slowly", Roy Lichtenstein

"Love", Robert Indiana

"The Bed", Henri de Toulouse-Lautrec

128

66

I loved her against reason,
against promise,
against peace, against hope,
against happiness,
against all discouragement
that could be.

99

**Pip,
Charles Dickens'
Great Expectations (1860)**

66

He looked at her
the way all women
want to be
looked at by a man.

99

**Nick Carraway,
F. Scott Fitzgerald's
The Great Gatsby (1925)**

"

The smile
is the beginning
of love.

"

Mother Teresa

66

Come ti vidi
M'innamorai,
E tu sorridi
Perchè lo sai.

When I saw you
I fell in love,
and you smiled
because you knew.

99

Giuseppe Verdi,
***Falstaff* (1893)**

132

66

If all else perished,
and he remained,
I should still continue to be;
and if all else remained,
and he were annihilated,
the universe would turn to a
mighty stranger.

99

Cathy, Emily Brontë's
***Wuthering Heights* (1847)**

CHAPTER
FIVE

"I Love You"

Will we ever get tired of
saying those three little words?
Or hearing them?

Probably not, since throughout
history we have been continually
coming up with new and ever more
heartfelt ways of expressing our
feelings to those we love.

As you'll probably find from the
declarations of love that follow,
however, often the simplest of words
capture our sentiments best...

66

When you realize
you want to spend the rest
of your life with somebody,
you want the rest
of your life to start as soon
as possible.

99

Harry Burns,
***When Harry Met Sally* (1989)**

66

I shall do one thing
in this life –
one thing certain – that is,
love you, and long for you,
and keep wanting you
till I die.

99

**Gabriel Oak,
Thomas Hardy's *Far from the
Madding Crowd* (1874)**

66

To me, you are perfect.

99

Mark,
Love Actually **(2003)**

According to Hallmark, approximately 145 million Valentine's Day cards are exchanged industry-wide each year, making Valentine's Day the second-largest holiday for giving greetings cards after Christmas.

I never wanted
to be your
whole life
– just your
**favourite
part.**

“

How do I love thee? Let me
count the ways.

I love thee to the depth and breadth
and height

My soul can reach, when feeling
out of sight

For the ends of being and ideal grace.

I love thee to the level of every day's

Most quiet need, by sun and
candle-light.

”

**Elizabeth Barrett Browning,
"Sonnet 43" (1846)**

66

I'm also just a girl,
standing in front of a boy,
asking him to love her.

99

Anna Scott,
Notting Hill (1999)

66

Every atom of your flesh is as
dear to me as my own:
in pain and sickness it would
still be dear.
Your mind is my treasure,
and if it were broken, it would be
my treasure still.

99

**Mr Rochester,
Charlotte Brontë's *Jane Eyre* (1847)**

The enduringly popular children's book Guess How Much I Love You *has sold over 47 million units and has been translated into 57 languages.*

“

I wanted it to be you,
I wanted it to be you
so badly.

”

Kathleen Kelly, *You've Got Mail* (1998)

I love you for

ALL

that you are,

ALL

that you have been and

ALL

that you're yet to be.

"

You should be kissed
and often,
and by someone who
knows how.

"

Rhett Butler,
***Gone With the Wind* (1939)**

> **66**
>
> I know you by heart.
> You are inside my heart.
>
> **99**

Sara,
Frances Hodgson Burnett's
***A Little Princess* (1905)**

It is actually possible to die from
a broken heart.

Taktsubo cardiomyopathy,
or "Broken heart syndrome",
can be brought on by extreme
stress and even the loss of
a loved one.

"

Bridegroom, dear to my heart,

Goodly is you beauty, honeysweet,

Lion, dear to my heart,

Goodly is your beauty, honeysweet.

"

"Istanbul #2461"
(AKA the world's oldest known love poem;
see page 33)

66

You had me at hello.

99

Dorothy Boyd, *Jerry Maguire* **(1996)**

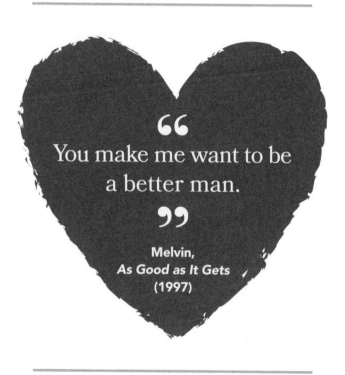

66

You make me want to be
a better man.

99

Melvin,
As Good as It Gets
(1997)

66

I love you very much,
probably more
than anybody could love
another person.

99

Henry, *50 First Dates* (2004)

66

I love you like a heart
needs a beat.

If ever two were one,
then surely we.

If ever man were loved by wife,
then thee.

99

**Anne Bradstreet,
"To My Dear and Loving Husband" (1678)**

66

You have stolen my heart,
my sister, my bride;

you have stolen my heart
with one glance of your eyes,

with one jewel of your
necklace.

99

**Song of Songs, 4:9,
New International Version**

66

I will return.
I will find you.
Love you.
Marry you.
And live without shame.

99

Robbie Turner,
Atonement **(2007)**

That all-important
first impression
actually has a time limit.

Four minutes

is all you have,
so don't waste them!

66

I like you very much.
Just as you are.

99

Mark Darcy,
***Bridget Jones's Diary* (2001)**

I saw that you
were
perfect
and so I loved you.

Then I saw that
you were
not perfect
and I loved you
even more.

Top 10 most
Romantic Cities
in the World

1. **Rome, Italy**
2. **Paris, France**
3. **Vilnius, Lithuania**
4. **Venice, Italy**
5. **Kyoto, Japan**
6. **Buenos Aires, Argentina**
7. **Marrakech, Morocco**
8. **Istanbul, Turkey**
9. **Bruges, Belgium**
10. **Québec City, Canada**

Source: **theculturetrip.com**

❝

Swoon. I'll catch you.

❞

Count Laszlo de Almásy,
The English Patient
(1996)

66

I have crossed oceans of time to find you.

99

Dracula,
Bram Stoker's Dracula
(1992)

Thinking of you keeps
me awake.

Dreaming of you keeps
me asleep.

Being with you keeps
me *alive.*

66

It seems right now
that all I've ever done
in my life
is making my way here
to you.

99

Robert Kincaid,
The Bridges of Madison County **(1995)**

When two people who are in love look each other in the eyes, within three minutes, their heartbeats will have synchronized.

"

In vain I have struggled.
It will not do.
My feelings will not be
repressed. You must allow
me to tell you how ardently
I admire and love you.

"

Mr Darcy,
Jane Austen's *Pride and Prejudice*
(1813)

"

I can't see anything I don't like about you.

"

Joel,
Eternal Sunshine of the
Spotless Mind **(2004)**

Cuddling creates the hormone oxytocin, which is a natural painkiller.

"

We'll always have Paris.

"

Rick Blaine, *Casablanca* (1942)

Give me a kiss and I'll
serenade you among the stars.

Give me your love
and I will pluck each star
to set at your feet.

"

O my Luve is like a red, red rose
That's newly sprung in June;
O my Luve is like the melody
That's sweetly played in tune.

So fair art thou, my bonnie lass,
So deep in luve am I;
And I will luve thee still, my dear,
Till a' the seas gang dry.

"

**Robert Burns,
"A Red, Red Rose" (1794)**

66

I come here with no
expectations, only to
profess, now that I am
at liberty to do so,
that my heart is and always
will be... yours.

99

Edward Ferrars,
Sense and Sensibility **(1995)**

*Those butterflies
in your stomach are actually
caused by adrenaline,
the same hormone that floods
your body in stressful,
fight-or-flight situations.*

66

If you're a bird, I'm a bird.

99

Noah,
The Notebook **(2004)**

I would
walk through the desert,
I would
walk down the aisle,
I would
swim all the oceans
just to see you

smile

Top 10

Honeymoon Destinations

1. The Maldives   2. USA
3. Italy   4. Bali
5. Mexico   6. The Caribbean
7. Mauritius   8. Thailand
9. Hawaii   10. Greece

Source: **Hitched.com**

66

You pierce my soul. I am half agony, half hope. Tell me not that I am too late, that such precious feelings are gone for ever. I offer myself to you again with a heart even more your own than when you almost broke it, eight years and a half ago. Dare not say that man forgets sooner than woman, that his love has an earlier death. I have loved none but you.

99

Captain Wentworth,
Jane Austen's *Persuasion* (1817)

I look at you and see
the rest of my life
in front of my eyes.

"

It has made me better loving
you... it has made me wiser,
and easier, and brighter. I used
to want a great many things before,
and to be angry that
I did not have them... Now
I really am satisfied, because I can't
think of anything better.

"

Gilbert Osmond, Henry James'
***The Portrait of a Lady* (1881)**

I love
you
every step
of the
way.

As well as
"the City of Light",
Paris
is also called
"the City of Love".

66

Remember,
we're madly in love,
so it's all right
to kiss me
any time
you feel like it.

99

Peeta,
The Hunger Games **(2012)**

66

I do love
nothing in the world
so well as
you – is not that
strange?

99

**Benedick,
Shakespeare's *Much Ado About Nothing*,
Act IV, Scene 1**

The heart shape can be traced back to a now-extinct species of giant fennel that grew in North Africa called the silphium, the seeds of which were shaped like a heart.

66

You are my heart,
my life,
my one and only
thought.

99

**Alleyne,
Arthur Conan Doyle's
The White Company (1891)**

66

I love you.
I knew it the minute
I met you.

99

Pat,
Silver Linings Playbook (2012)

*Forever
is a
long time,
but I
wouldn't
mind spending it* **by your side.**

"

With the whole world
crumbling,
we pick this time
to fall in love.

"

Ilsa Lund,
Casablanca **(1942)**

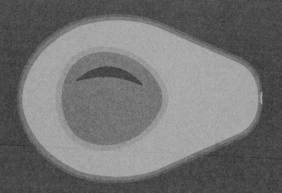

Top 10
Aphrodisiac Foods

1. Pomegranates
2. Avocados
3. Bananas
4. Salmon
5. Chocolate
6. Watermelon
7. Oysters
8. Red wine
9. Pumpkin seeds
10. Spinach

Source: **thegentlemansjournal.com**

66

Doubt thou the stars are fire;

Doubt that the sun doth move;

Doubt truth to be a liar;

But never doubt I love.

99

Hamlet,
Shakespeare's *Hamlet*,
Act II, Scene 2

66

Love.
The reason I dislike
that word is that it means
too much for me,
far more than you can
understand.

99

Anna,
Leo Tolstoy's *Anna Karenina*
(1877)

Based on the amount of adaptations
and performances, Shakespeare's

Romeo & Juliet

is the most well-known
love story ever
told.